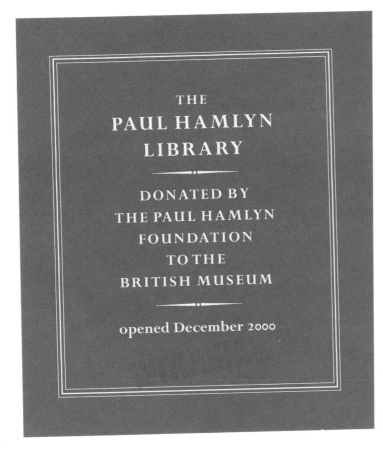

DAILY LIFE

Stewart Ross

WAYLAND

ANCIENT GREECE
Daily Life
Gods and Goddesses
Greek Theatre
The Original Olympics

Editor: Elizabeth Gogerly
Design: Stonecastle Graphics Ltd
Consultant: Dr Angus Bowie

First published in 1999 by
Wayland (Publishers) Ltd, 61 Western Road,
Hove, East Sussex, BN3 1JD

Find Wayland on the Internet at http://www.wayland.co.uk

The quotations in this book have been translated and, in some cases, adapted from their translations, to make them easier to read.

British Library Cataloguing in Publication Data
Ross, Stewart
  Daily life. – (Ancient Greece)
  1. Greece – Civilization – To 146 B.C. – Juvenile literature
  I. Title
  938

ISBN 0 7502 2489 4

Photographic acknowledgements
The publishers would like to thank the following sources for providing photographs:
AKG London 7, 11, 19, 23, 25, 26, 32, 35, 37, 39, 40; **Ancient Art and Architecture Collection** 17, 22, 28, 41; C.M. Dixon 4, 14, 15, 20, 25, 30, 31, 34, 43, 44 ; **e.t archive** 33, 45; **Bridgeman / Ashmolean Museum** 18; **Robert Harding** 44; **Michael Holford** (cover), 8, 21, 24, 29, 36; **Tony Stone** 38-39; **Wayland Picture Library** 5, 45/**British Museum** 7 (bottom), 12-13, 14, 32/**Ashmolean Museum** 9.

Illustration: John Yates **Map designs:** Hardlines

Reproduction by Pageturn Ltd.
Printed and bound by Eurografica, Italy

CONTENTS

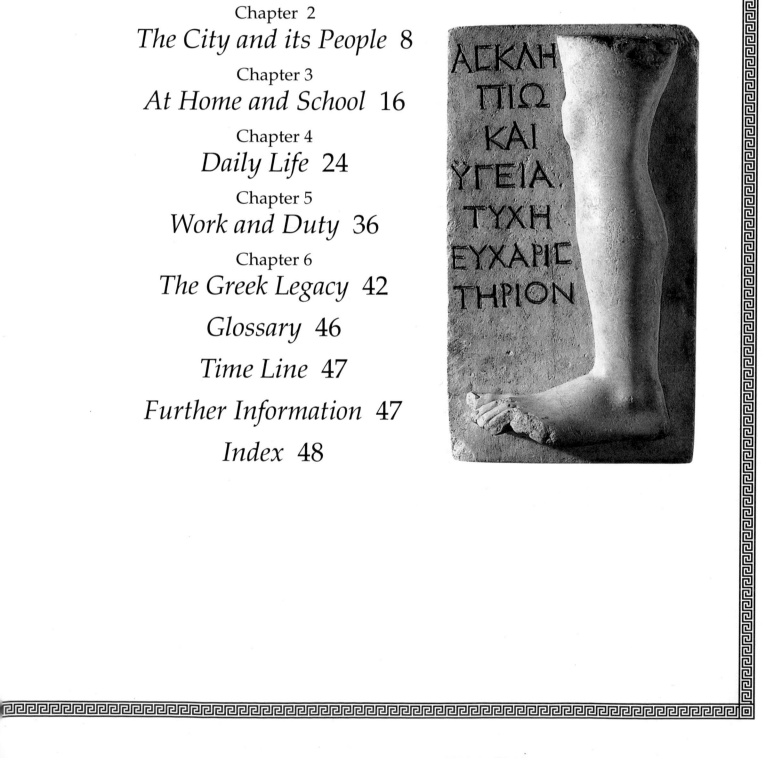

1 Into the Agora

Hegeso lies in bed listening to the noises of the dawn. Her mother is still asleep beside her, breathing quietly. From the room next door comes the sound of her father's snores. A goat bleats in the yard outside. Up on the farmhouse roof, a thrush sings its welcome to the rising sun.

Suddenly, Hegeso remembers!

She jumps up and runs wildly around the house, waking everyone with her cries. It's the day she has been looking forward to for ages. For the first time ever, her father is taking Hegeso and her brother Dexileos into Athens with him.

Off to market, about 380 BC. The farmer is using his cheeses as a saddle for his mule.

On the road

Hegeso's father is a farmer. With the help of three slaves, he runs a small farm at the foot of Mount Agaleos, some 16 km north-west of the city. About once a month he loads up their mule with goats' cheese and takes it into Athens to sell. Normally, he is accompanied only by the slave, Manes. But today he has agreed that once – just once – Hegeso and Dexileos can come too.

An hour after sunrise, they are on their way. They soon leave the farm track and join the Sacred Way, the main road between their home in the mountains and Athens.

Into the city

They cross a large river and Hegeso's father points out the *Acropolis* in the far distance. This is the rocky peak at the heart of the city. Its magnificent buildings gleam in the sunlight.

Soon they reach the outskirts of Athens. The busy side streets are full of noisy workshops and there seems to be lots of people.

Hegeso and Dexileos stare in amazement. Aged ten and eight, they have spent their entire lives in the countryside. They have never experienced anything like the sights, noises and smells of the great city. It's amazing! And rather frightening, too. Hegeso grabs Manes's hand and holds on tightly.

> *'Whoever said that farming is the foundation of all the arts, is quite correct. When all is well on the farms, all is well elsewhere.'*
>
> Xenophon in *Oeconomicus*, about 370 BC.

Υ
Φ
Χ
Ψ

ΘΙΚΛΜΝΞΟΠΡΣΤΥΦΧΨΩ

The Acropolis of Athens, almost as magnificent today as it was in Hegeso's time.

The Agora

Following the Sacred Way, the family pass a huge cemetery and enter the city by a large gate. As they approach the main square called the *Agora*, the street becomes still more crowded with carts and people.

Hegeso thinks the Agora the most fascinating place she has ever seen. It is surrounded by temples and other fine buildings, and jammed with shops, stalls and counters. She follows her father towards the stall of a cheese seller. All of a sudden, she sees a girl about her own age. She smiles. The girl smiles back, then vanishes into the crowd.

A map of ancient Athens. The city was surrounded by high walls and could be entered only through one of the ten gates.

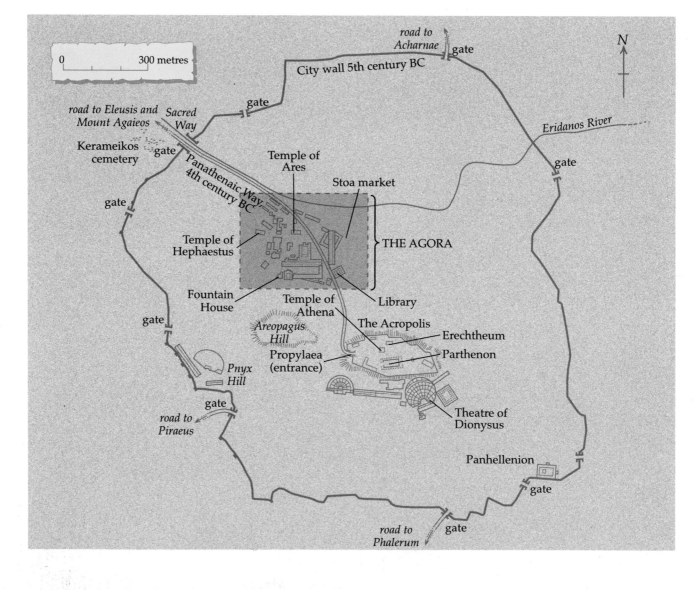

A family visit

The girl Hegeso saw is Lysimache. She and her sister, Praxinoa, live to the north of Athens. Accompanied by four household slaves, Lysimache and Praxinoa are crossing the city with their mother to visit their grandmother. They rarely leave the house, and are just as excited as Hegeso and Dexileos by their journey through the city.

Lysimache and Praxinoa live in great comfort. But as is the custom in ancient Greece, they spend most of their time in the *gynaikeion*, the women's quarters on the first floor of their large house. They see little of their wealthy father. He is always busy with his duties as a citizen.

> 'Everyone likes to wander round the city and drop in at the barber's or cobbler's for a chat ... and they always chose somewhere in the Agora rather than a place on the outskirts of the city.'
>
> From a speech by Lysias, about 400 BC.

Across the city

That morning, a slave girl had dressed Lysimache and Praxinoa in their best tunics and given them breakfast. Before leaving their mother had warned the girls not to speak to anybody and not to stare about them. Respectable girls, she had insisted, are modest at all times.

Now they are in the street, the girls are heading towards the Acropolis. Lysimache remembers what her mother told her but she cannot help looking around at the sights of the wonderful city. She longs to speak with the smiling simply-dressed girl she sees in the Agora but Lysimache knows she should not. Instead she tries to imagine how different the other girl's life must be.

Lysimache and Praxinoa were wealthy girls rather like the pair in this statuette.

This painted dish shows a shoemaker at his workbench. This was just one of the many kinds of trades that took place in the Agora in ancient Athens.

2 The City and its People

Hegeso and Lysimache lived in Greece, about 2,450 years ago. Greece was not a true country then, even though the Greeks did think of themselves as a nation. It was divided into a number of small states, each centred around a city. The ancient word for Greece was Hellas, and the people living there called themselves Hellenes.

The people who eventually called themselves Greeks came into the peninsula from about 2000 BC. By the eighth century BC they had built up a flourishing civilization. A civilization that lasted until the second century BC, when Greece became part of the Roman Empire. Hegeso and Praxinoa lived during a time which is now called *Classical Greece*. Lasting for 150 years, from about 480–330 BC, this was when ancient Greek civilization was at its peak.

Archaeologists uncover the remains of Athens' main square, the Agora. Archaeology is vitally important in helping us to understand how the ancient Greeks lived.

Ancient glory

We are fascinated by ancient Greece because the roots of much of our government, literature, science and learning go back to that time.

The Greeks have had more influence on our civilization than any other people in history. The very word history comes from the ancient Greek language! Without realizing it, we also use other words that come from the ancient Greek language, such as school, and mathematics.

This tablet is from ancient Crete which was part of the Greek empire. The Greek letters on this tablet were scratched onto the wet clay. When it dried the writing could not be removed.

How do we know?

Historians use all sorts of sources to build up a picture of what life was like in ancient Greece. The Greeks were great writers. Although most of their literature has been lost, what remains give us valuable clues about the way they lived and thought.

Pictures, particularly those on Greek pottery, and other objects discovered by *archaeologists* also help us to find out what daily life was like for the ancient Greeks. Buildings and finds, such as weapons, coins and jewellery, help us to form a vision of this wonderful world. Now, after years of research, we have quite a good idea of what it was like to live when Hegeso and Lysimache were alive.

'Future ages will wonder at us, as the present age wonders at us now.'

The Athenian statesman Pericles in a funeral speech during the Peloponnesian War, 431–404 BC.

Υ Φ Χ Ψ

ΘΙΚΛΜΝΞΟΠΡΣΤΥΦΧΨΩ

The city-states

A city-state in ancient Greece was known as a *polis*, from which we get our word 'politics'. Most city-states consisted of a walled city, and surrounding countryside and agricultural land.

Although all the city-states of ancient Greece shared the same language, and much of the same culture, the way they were governed varied widely. And each state chose its own god as its protector.

Attica

In the Classical period, when Hegeso and Lysimache were alive, Attica was by far the wealthiest and most important polis. Its chief city, Athens, was one of the greatest cities of the ancient world.

The world of ancient Greece, showing Attica at its centre. The map makes it clear why sea trade was so important to the city of Athens and the territory around it.

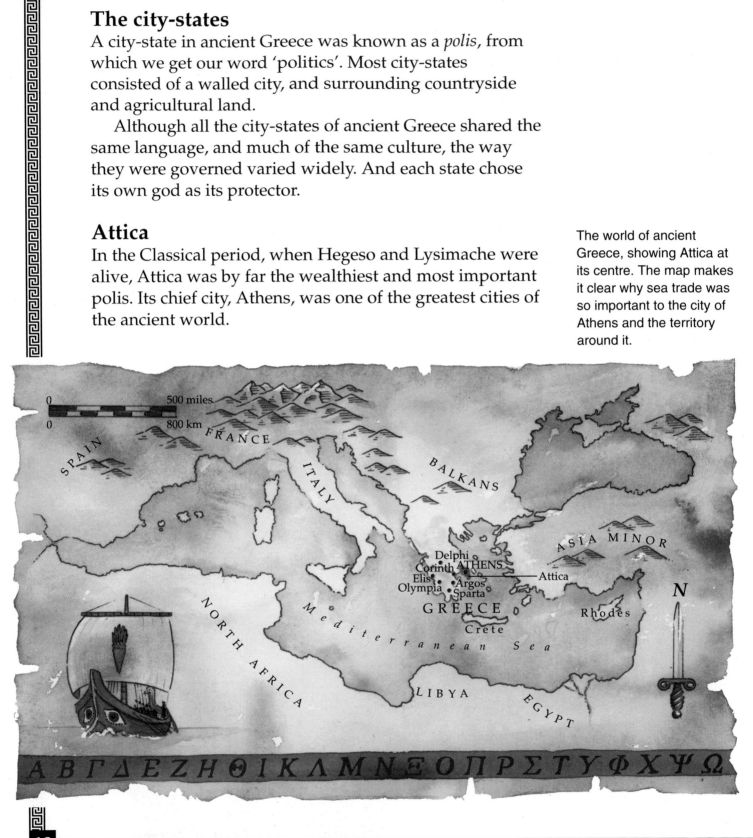

Shaped like a triangle, with the sea on two sides, Attica covered about 1,600 square km. The area controlled by Attica was actually much larger than this because it had colonies right around the Aegean Sea. In the middle of the fifth century BC the population of Attica was about 300,000. Because much of its land was of poor agricultural quality, Attica's wealth depended on manufacture and trade.

Athens

More than 1,600m across, with the large rocky outcrop (the Acropolis) at the centre, the city was surrounded by 6.5 km of walls. Massive walls also protected the main road to the city's port, Piraeus.

Athens came to dominate Greece after the wars fought against Persia, 490–479 BC. Athens organized the Greek states against the Persian invaders, defeating the enemy at Marathon in 490 BC. Following the Greek naval victory at Salamis (480 BC), Athens entered its 'golden age'. However, this supremacy did not last long. After the Peloponnesian Wars with Sparta (431-404 BC), Athens never fully recovered its former magnificence.

'The skillfully handled Greek ships surrounded the Persians and attacked inwards. Many ships turned over and the sea disappeared beneath blood and wreckage.'

Aeschylus, The Persians, about 418 BC, describing the Battle of Salamis.

ΤΥΦΧΨ

ΘΙΚΛΜΝΞΟΠΡΣΤΥΦΧΨΩ

Fighting between Greek foot-soldiers and Persian cavalry on a fifth century Greek vase. The Greeks often fought almost naked.

11

The government of Athens

During the fifth century BC, Athens, as Attica is often known, developed a system of government known as democracy which means that the government was elected by the people. At a time when all other states and neighbouring countries were ruled by a monarchy or by small privileged groups, the Athenians ruled themselves. It was a unique idea and a great source of their strength.

Supreme power rested with the *Assembly*. It met 40 times a year in Athens, and was open to all adult male citizens. It business was guided by a Council of 500 citizens, chosen by *lot* from the ten tribes of Attica. Day-to-day decisions were made by the *Prytaneis*, the inner council of 50.

Citizens of Athens casting their votes at an election. Slaves and foreigners were not permitted to become citizens, so power rested in the hands of a small minority of residents.

Citizens

Democracy in Attica was not like a modern democracy. Only adult male citizens had a say in the government. A citizen was someone born of a marriage between two citizens. Very occasionally, outsiders could be made citizens by special decree. Otherwise, the citizen body remained a fixed and privileged few.

Women, men under the age of 18, foreigners living in Athens (known as *metics)* and slaves were excluded. This meant that, although the total population of Attica was perhaps 300,000, only about 45,000 could attend the Assembly.

Demes

All citizens belonged to a complicated network of groups. As well as their family, they were part of a kind of brotherhood, known as a *phratry*. They were also members of religious, dining and sporting organizations.

For administration, Attica was divided up into *phylai*, *trittyes* and *demes*. There were ten phylai, each consisting of three trittyes – one city area, one coastal area and one inland area. The 170 demes were the smallest units. Each one was supervised by a *demarchos* who was elected by the citizens of that deme for one year.

> *'We call our system of government a democracy because power rests with everyone, not with a tiny minority.'*
>
> Pericles' funeral speech, delivered in the winter of 431–430 BC.

Metics

Metics were the 50,000 foreigners living in Attica. They played no part in the government, but paid only light taxes. They were also free to own slaves.

Most metics were businessmen or craftsmen, such as metal-workers and weavers. A few were teachers or doctors. The Athenians realized that metics were valuable members of the community, and the punishment for murdering a metic was death.

Slavery

Slavery was an accepted part of Athenian life. Over half the population of Attica were slaves. They did mostly manual work, giving citizens time for their duties, their work and their leisure.

Slaves were seen as objects. They were prisoners of war or kidnap victims, and could be bought in the Agora slave market for between 150 and 300 *drachmas* (at that time, a soldier or craftsman received about 1 drachma a day). Most slaves received no pay. Their children belonged to their master, and runaway slaves were branded with a red-hot iron.

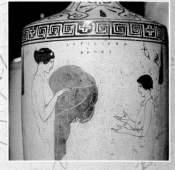

A woman and her maid. Serving girls were slaves. They received no wages and had to do precisely as they were told.

In Attica, the slaves' lives gradually improved. They were protected against unnecessary cruelty and, towards the end of the Classical period, some thinkers were even suggesting that slavery itself might be wrong.

Slaves' work

Most citizens owned slaves. Hegeso's father had two who helped in the house, and three farm slaves. Lysimache's father was much wealthier, with a dozen slaves doing the housework under a slave master, who was himself a slave. The most important were the doorkeeper, gardener, cooks, secretary and maids.

The state owned slaves, too. Slave clerks and minor officials were paid a salary and allowed to marry. The best-known state slaves were the 1,000 *Scythian* archers employed as Athen's police force. Life was hardest for slave corn grinders and miners in the silver mines. The miners worked in terrible conditions and punishments for disobedience were severe. The death rate among them was very high.

'The human race has certain inferior individuals ...
.Nature has destined such people to become slaves, for they are ideally suited to obeying.'
Aristotle, *Politics*, about 340 BC.

ΘΙΚΛΜΝΞΟΠΡΣΤΥΦΧΨΩ

Slaves hurrying to a banquet with food for the guests.

3 At Home and School

The city of Athens has been rebuilt many times since the Classical period, and the remains of the ancient city lie many metres below the present street level. This means that we only have an idea of what a house was like. The houses excavated by archaeologists are small and simple, so we can only guess what larger houses, such as Lysimache's wealthy father's house, would have been like.

It was probably two stories high, with flat roofs. Bigger houses were probably built round a courtyard. The women's quarters were probably on the upper floor. There was a kitchen and bathroom, but the fire used for cooking was lit outside and brought indoors when needed. We also know that the walls were thin, because there are reports of robbers digging through the walls of the house!

An artist's impression of what a large Greek house might have looked like. Only the best houses were built round a courtyard.

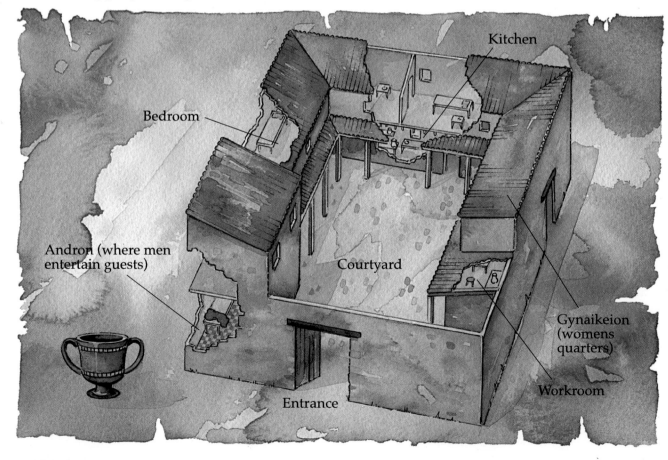

Kitchen

Bedroom

Andron (where men entertain guests)

Courtyard

Gynaikeion (womens quarters)

Workroom

Entrance

Country houses

As far as we can tell, farmhouses and other houses in the country were quite small. This means that Hegeso's house was probably only one-storey high. The rooms were probably arranged round a courtyard, which had a well in the centre.

As in the town, the women's and men's rooms were probably separate. The kitchen and bathroom may have been next to each other, so that the bathroom was kept warm in the winter. Chamber pots were used instead of lavatories, and there was no running water. The walls were most probably plain plaster, with nails or wooden pegs for hanging things on.

Furniture and equipment

Greek houses were much less cluttered than modern houses. Furniture was simple and consisted of beds and couches, chairs and stools, lamps, chests for storage and three-legged tables.

Cooking was done on an open fire, using metal pots. Food was served on wooden plates, but without forks or spoons. Earthenware jars of many shapes and designs were used for storing food and drink.

This beautiful bronze vessel, probably a charcoal burner, was made in the fourth century BC. Bronze, a mixture of copper and tin, was widely used in ancient Greece because it is tough but easy to work and it does not rust.

'Let me tell you .. that my tiny house has an upper storey. The rooms are arranged the same upstairs and downstairs, with the women's quarters on one floor and the men's on the other.'

Lysias, On the Murder of Eratosthenes, about 400 BC.

Θ Ι Κ Λ Μ Ν Ξ Ο Π Ρ Σ Τ Υ Φ Χ Ψ Ω

Families

Athens was a man's world. Men ran the city-state and organized everything to suit themselves. Families were very important to the ancient Greeks, but their idea of a family was quite different to ours.

The father was the head of the family, and everyone had to do as he said. In some families, the men did not see much of the women. Wives stayed at home and ran the household. A husband could divorce his wife if she was unfaithful or if they had no children. It was much more difficult for a wife to divorce her husband.

Marriage

Marriages were arranged by fathers, close male relatives or guardians. They were not romantic unions between two people who had fallen in love. Love might grow between a married couple, but the main purpose of a marriage was to produce children to continue the family name and honour their parents after they had died.

The marriage ceremony was in two parts. First came the betrothal, or engagement. This was an agreement that the marriage would take place. The bride-to-be may not have been even present. Weddings often took place in the winter on the day of a full moon. The central part of the ceremony was a procession taking the bride to her husband's house.

A Greek bride washing at an indoor fountain as she prepares for her wedding.

Women

Compared with women today, women in Classical Attica lived very restricted lives. Respectable young women rarely left their women's quarters, known as the *gynaikeion*. Lysimache's mother went out occasionally to attend a festival. Otherwise, she would have stayed at home with the keys of the house at her waist as a symbol of her authority.

Women from poorer families, especially in the country, enjoyed greater freedom. When one of their slaves was ill, Hegeso's mother would probably have helped with farm work. The least restricted women were the wives of metics.

A mother and her child. The woman is wearing the baggy tunic known as a *peplos.* Like all respectable Greek women, she has her head covered.

A betrothal scene from Menander's play *Periceiromene.* Pataecus is the person legally responsible for the girl he is giving away. Polemon is the suitor.

PATAECUS *I give you this girl so that she may produce children in marriage.*

POLEMON *I accept her.*

PATAECUS *I agree to provide her with a dowry of three talents.*

POLEMON *I accept that as well. Thank you.*

Σ Τ Υ Φ Χ Ψ

ΑΒΓΔΕΖΗΘΙΚΛΜΝΞΟΠΡΣΤΥΦΧΨΩ

A new baby

Citizens did not generally have big families. A wife could have an abortion, with her husband's consent. Citizens would also rid themselves of an unwanted baby by placing it in a clay pot, which also acted as the tomb, and leaving it to die.

Before a baby was born, the house was daubed with pitch to ward off evil spirits. The birth was attended by several women, some of whom were midwives. After the birth, an olive branch was hung outside the house if the child was a boy, and a strip of woollen cloth for a girl. A special ceremony was held about a week later. Three days after that, the parents made a sacrifice to the gods and named the child.

The ancient Greeks' attitude to childbirth was practical rather than romantic. This early sixth century tablet reads 'Hermon wants to know to which god he should pray for his wife to bare useful children.'

Children

Boys were in the care of their mothers until they went to school. Girls remained with their mothers until they left home to get married. New-born babies were wrapped in tight *swaddling clothes* and breast fed by their mothers. They often slept in wicker cradles and were entertained with lullabies.

Boys seem to have worn few clothes about the house. Girls dressed in simple tunics. Many children are pictured wearing a string of charms to ward off bad luck and illness.

Toys and games

Like many ancient Greek children, Hegeso and Dexileos had all sorts of toys to play with when they were young. Hegeso and Dexileos's father made them rattles and a tiny chariot that could be pulled along on a piece of string. They also liked the animal figures and dolls that Manes the slave made for them.

When they were older, they played ball games outside the house. Sometimes, when they were bored, they took their pet weasel, Pipos, into the barn and watched him catch mice!

'*Sleep, O my children, sleep in peace and calm.*
Brother with brother, sleep my lovely boys,
Blest in both your slumbers and your waking.'

A lullaby by the poet Theocritus, about 280 BC

Τ
Υ
Φ
Χ
Ψ

Θ Ι Κ Λ Μ Ν Ξ Ο Π Ρ Σ Τ Υ Φ Χ Ψ Ω

A child's doll made of pottery. The arms and legs are held on with pins so they can move.

To school

In Athens citizens could only attend fee-paying private schools. The city paid for boys whose fathers had died for their country. As there were no girls' schools, girls had to learn what they could from their mothers or from an educated slave.

Boys were taught at home until the age of seven. Then, if there was a school nearby, they went to daily classes. Each pupil was accompanied by his *paedagogos*. This was a household slave who watched over the boy's progress and punished him if he was lazy or misbehaved. Pupils sat on stools before the teacher, each with their paedagogos watching in the background. The school day lasted from dawn to dusk, with no weekends off or school holidays. The only breaks from lessons were during festivals.

Writing

A schoolboy's main equipment consisted of a wooden board, covered in wax, and a stylus. This was a sharp rod, like a pen, for writing on the wax. When they were older, they wrote on a kind of paper, known as *papyrus*. Ink came in solid blocks which had to be mixed with water before it could be used.

A girl reading from a scroll. There were no girls' schools in ancient Greece, so girls had to pick up what education they could from their mothers or from slaves.

'If a child obeys his teachers, that's fine. If he doesn't, he is brought into shape with threats and blows, like a piece of wood that is bent or warped.'

Plato, recording the words of Protagoras, fifth century BC.

ΘΙΚΛΜΝΞΟΠΡΣΤΥΦΧΨΩ

Subjects

The first two or three years were spent learning to read and write. Pupils then moved on to learning passages by heart, especially the works of the famous Greek poet Homer. Mathematics was very difficult because the Greeks used the letters of the alphabet for numbers, but had no way of writing zero.

Music and sport were also important to the ancient Greeks. They considered music the foundation of all culture - the very word 'music' comes from the Muses, the Greek goddesses who guided all arts and learning. Pupils learned to play the *aulos*, a kind of flute, and the *kithara*, a *lyre*. Physical education began at the age of 12 with boxing and athletics.

Learning to play the kithara, or lyre. Music was an essential part of a Greek boy's education.

4 Daily Life

Everything the Greeks made came from natural substances. They used stone, clay and marble for building, iron, tin and copper for tools and weapons, and wool, leather, linen, cotton and silk for clothing. Synthetic substances, such as plastics and nylon, were unknown. Cotton and silk were luxuries.

Male dress

Greek men were quite used to being seen with no clothes on. They met together, naked, in the public baths, and most athletes competed in the nude.

The basic item of male dress was the woollen tunic, either the everyday *exomis*, draped over one shoulder, or the *chiton*, worn on both shoulders and gathered in folds about the waist. Both were tied round the waist with a girdle.

In cold weather men wore a large rectangle of wool, known as a *himation*, which was carefully draped over the left shoulder. They went barefoot indoors, but put on leather sandals when going out. Most men had beards and quite short hair.

Two golden rings. The snake ring may have been worn to bring good health, as the snake was a symbol of healing.

'*Isomachus noticed that his wife was wearing make-up. She had white lead on her face, to make it even whiter, and red juice on her cheeks. She was in high-heels, too!*'

From Xenophon's *Oeconomicus*, about 380 BC.

ΑΒΓΔΕΖΗΘΙΚΛΜΝΞΟΠΡΣΤΥΦΧΨΩ

Female dress

Women's clothing was also based on a large rectangle of wool or linen. This was made into a *peplos*. This was a type of open tunic which could be pinned on each shoulder or sewn up to make a dress. A large peplos could be pulled over the head and worn like a hood. It could also be worn with or without a girdle.

Like men, women wore sandals outdoors, and in cold weather women wore shawls. Wealthy women often carried parasols to keep off the sun and rain.

At the time of the Persian wars, both men and women wore jewellery. In Classical times, men wore only a signet ring. Women had a wide choice of necklaces, bracelets, earrings and anklets, made of precious metal, amber, jade or ivory. They wore eye-liner, face make-up and often dyed their hair.

A statue of the goddess Kore, also known as Persephone. The way she wears her peplos in elegant folds was typical of wealthy Greek women.

Meal times

The Greeks took their main meal between five and six o'clock in the evening.

Because the ancient Greeks had no accurate way of telling the time, they organized their days by the Sun. The hours of daylight were divided into early morning, late morning, afternoon and evening. Appointments and meal times were often arranged according to the length of a shadow cast by a long stick, a time stick.

By the time the ancient Greeks ate their main meal the shadow from a time stick might be between two to six metres long.

A Symposion, or drinking party. The guests were all men, although slave girls sometimes served the food, played music and danced for their entertainment.

The Symposion

The best-known Greek meal was the *Symposion*, literally meaning 'drinking party'. The modern equivalent would be a dinner party. It was held in a private house and only male guests were invited. They sat or lay on couches and had food and drink brought to them by slaves.

The Symposion began with the meal and continued with drinking and entertainment. Fashionable dinners sometimes included delicacies such as roasted songbird, snails, fish roe (eggs), tuna and even grasshoppers. After dinner the guests told stories and held discussions, recited poetry and enjoyed the music and dancing of slave girls.

> *'I am not keen to hear the man who drinks his wine
> And talks of serious things like war all the time.'*
> From the poet Anacreon, mid sixth century BC.

HΘIKΛMNΞOΠPΣTYΦXΨΩ

Food and drink

Most Greeks ate a healthy and well-balanced diet. Their main food was bread, with which they would eat green vegetables, beans, lentils, eggs, cheese, garlic, olives and olive oil.

Meat was expensive and rarely eaten but fish was plentiful and a rich source of protein for the ancient Greeks. Meals were flavoured with herbs and aniseed.

The ancient Greeks enjoyed their fruit too, and figs and grapes grew well on their hillsides. Sweet dishes were often made with delicious honey.

Breakfast and lunch were light meals, consisting of bread, wine and perhaps cheese or olives. The evening meal was fuller and often accompanied by quantities of wine. Water, goat's milk and wine were drunk from pottery cups. Wine was served from leather bottles, and stored in clay jars known as *pithoi*.

Keeping clean

The Greeks were keen on personal hygiene.
Women washed at home, from a bowl or
stone fountain, while men liked to meet in
public baths. The favourite bath time was in
the hour before the evening meal. Public
baths and swimming pools, with their steam
rooms and cold plunge pools, became
popular meeting places.

Soap was unknown to the ancient Greeks.
Instead they washed with a special kind of
clay and other rough substances. Afterwards,
they liked to rub oil over their bodies and have
it scraped off by a slave, leaving the skin
clean and tingling.

Keeping fit

Most ancient Greek men liked to keep
themselves in good shape. Even old men exercised
to keep themselves fit. The Greeks made frequent use
of the *gymnasion*. The ancient Greeks admired and
respected people with physical strength so visits to the
gymnasion were as much about boosting their social
standing as making themselves attractive.

Lysimache's father exercised in the *palaestra*. This was a
large, square, open-air sports ground, with changing
rooms and bath houses round the edge.

There were regular
sports meetings all
over Greece, the most
famous of which was
the Olympic Games.
A returning
champion was
greeted as a hero and
rewarded with feasts,
honours and presents.

Women washing at home.
Public bath houses were
for men only.

*'That little monkey Cleigenes, the most wicked
bath attendant who ever lived!'*
From Aristophanes's play Frogs, about 410 BC.

Υ
Φ
Χ
Ψ

ΘΙΚΛΜΝΞΟΠΡΣΤΥΦΧΨΩ

Sports and games

Sporting festivals in ancient Greece involved all kinds of events. There were running races over various distances, horse races, long-jump, and discus throwing competitions, boxing and wrestling matches – and sometimes even a race when the competitors dressed in armour!

Other outdoor pursuits included fishing, hunting and various ball games. The Greeks loved gambling and bet on horse races and cock fights, or on simple games with dice.

Greek boxers with their hands bound with ox hide. As a fight did not take place in a ring and could last for hours, broken bones were common.

Religion

The ancient Greeks believed in many gods and goddesses. They thought the gods were rather like super-humans, who controlled everything, from the growing of crops to victory in war and the success of a marriage. Religion was therefore tremendously important, touching all aspects of everyday life.

Zeus was king of the gods, and he lived on Mount Olympus. Many ancient Greeks had an altar to Zeus in their homes.

Worship

Greek worship involved prayer, sacrifice and purification. Prayers usually meant asking the gods for something or praising them. Prayers were made either standing up with the arms outstretched, or lying face-down on the ground.

Because the gods and goddesses were thought to be rather like humans, they were offered things which humans valued. These might be animals, such as sheep, oxen or deer, which were sacrificed and burned. Other offerings included honey cakes and corn. Purification was the cleansing of body and soul which took place at various special ceremonies.

A bronze statue of the god Zeus, about to throw a thunderbolt. Zeus was also known as the the god of sky and thunder.

Temples and festivals

The ancient Greeks honoured their deities with hundreds of temples and statues. The temples were usually very grand buildings, with roofs supported by rows of spectacular columns. The most famous statue of the goddess Athena stood on the Acropolis. Made of gold and ivory, it stood almost nine metres high.

There was a whole range of religious festivals. Three of the largest in Athens were:
• the Eleusinian Mysteries, held at the end of the summer in honour of Demeter, the goddess of crops, and her daughter Persephone.

Awesome even today, the temple of Athena on the acropolis (fortress) of Lindos on the isle of Rhodes.

• the Great Pan which was held every four years near the middle of the summer in honour of Athena, the goddess of wisdom, art and war.

• the City Dionysia, a spring festival held for Dionysus, the god of the grapevine, which incorporated drama.

Oracles

An *oracle* was a place where Greeks could ask their deities for advice. The most famous oracle was at the city of Delphi where priests of Apollo answered questions. Their predictions were carefully worded, so that they would be right whatever happened!

An ancient Greek prayer:

'If I have honoured you with burnt sacrifices of the heavy thighs of bulls and goats, answer my prayer.'

ΥΦΧΨ

ΘΙΚΛΜΝΞΟΠΡΣΤΥΦΧΨΩ

Medicine

Greek medicine was a mixture of folk remedies, superstition and science. Men and women had always noticed the healing effects of certain plants and herbs and doctors used them to heal the sick. But just as important were prayers, offerings and sacrifices to Asclepius, the god of healing.

There were all sorts of doctors in Athens, but the most reliable had been trained on the island of Cos, which boasted the best medical school in the region. Led by Hippocrates, the founder of the school, these doctors tried to find out how the body worked. They then tried to identify the different kinds of diseases and medicines to cure them.

Death and burial

In Greek mythology the dead crossed the River Styx to the Underworld. This was the kingdom of Hades. Because the ancient Greeks believed in this passage to another world, a funeral and its preparations were very important.

The body was perfumed with oils and laid out at home in clean clothes, with a garland of flowers round the head. A coin was sometimes put in the mouth to pay the Styx ferryman. The dead person's most valued possessions were also placed in their coffin. The family shaved their heads and wore mourning clothes. Then there was much ritual weeping and wailing.

Thanks, Aesculapius! This plaque was made to thank Aesculapius, the god of healing, for making a patient's leg better.

Part of the oath sworn by new doctors in ancient Greece. It is said to have been devised by Hippocrates.

'I swear by Apollo ... that whatever house I enter, I will do so only to help the sick ...'

ΘΙΚΛΜΝΞΟΠΡΣΤΥΦΧΨΩ

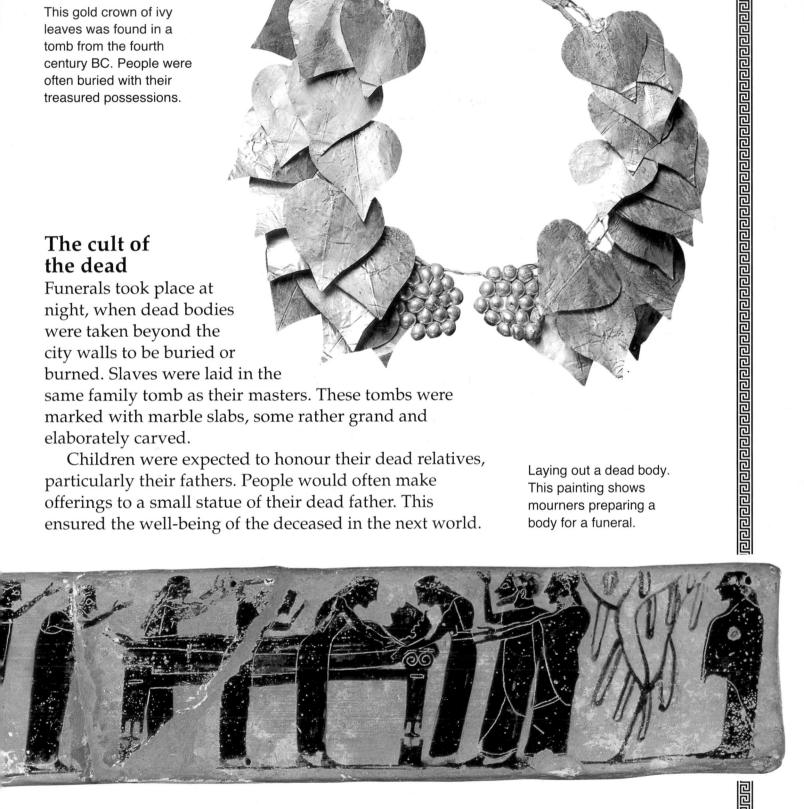

This gold crown of ivy leaves was found in a tomb from the fourth century BC. People were often buried with their treasured possessions.

The cult of the dead

Funerals took place at night, when dead bodies were taken beyond the city walls to be buried or burned. Slaves were laid in the same family tomb as their masters. These tombs were marked with marble slabs, some rather grand and elaborately carved.

Children were expected to honour their dead relatives, particularly their fathers. People would often make offerings to a small statue of their dead father. This ensured the well-being of the deceased in the next world.

Laying out a dead body. This painting shows mourners preparing a body for a funeral.

The law

The people of Athens had great respect for the law. They believed it was what held the city together. To break the law was to go against the will of the citizens, because their will was the law.

The law was upheld by individuals and by the police force of archers known as the Scythian archers. It was controlled by 'the eleven' which was a group of magistrates. The state could not prosecute anyone. A person accused of a crime, even a crime against Athens itself, had to be taken to court by another individual.

Soldiers like this Scythian archer made up the Athenian police force.

Courts

The Athenian system of law courts was extremely complicated. The courts were supervised by magistrates who were citizens. The decision about whether someone was guilty or not was made by a *jury* of fellow citizens. The jury might contain as many as 2001 men! Really serious cases about the security of Athens might be heard by the whole *Assembly*.

In court, the person bringing the case, the plaintiff, and the accused both presented their cases. They could employ professionals to write their speeches for them. The jury was not allowed to interrupt although it might let its feelings be known by murmuring. When both sides had finished, the jury voted on whether the accused was guilty or not. There was always an odd number of people on the jury, so there was always a majority vote.

Punishment

Punishments varied widely. There were different punishments for citizens, metics and slaves. Those who confessed to a murder did not even get to court, they were executed on the spot. Those found guilty of murder in a trial werc hung by the hands, wrists and feet outside the city walls, and left to die.

Other punishments included fines, confiscation of property, banishment and, rarely, imprisonment. Only slaves might be whipped and branded.

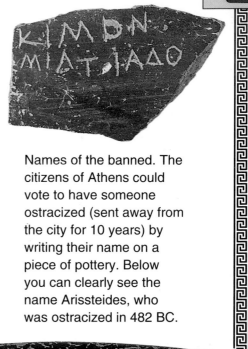

Names of the banned. The citizens of Athens could vote to have someone ostracized (sent away from the city for 10 years) by writing their name on a piece of pottery. Below you can clearly see the name Arissteides, who was ostracized in 482 BC.

'*I will vote according to the laws and decrees of the Assembly and Council. Where there are no laws, I will find the most just answer, without showing any favours ...*'

Part of the oath probably sworn by Athenian jurymen.

Υ Φ Χ Ψ

ΑΒΓΔΕΖΗΘΙΚΛΜΝΞΟΠΡΣΤΥΦΧΨΩ

5 Work and Duty

The power and wealth of Athens depended on the city's businesses. Many citizens had jobs, but they felt no disgrace in increasing their wealth through trade. Lysimache's father made money by importing corn from Scythia, to the north of the Black Sea. He did not need to have a job and would have felt it was beneath him to work for a wage. Wages, citizens believed, took away their freedom. The ideal life was said to be that of the independent small farmer.

A Greek merchant ship about 540 BC. Ships like these, traded all over the Mediterranean, and were the key to Athens's wealth and power.

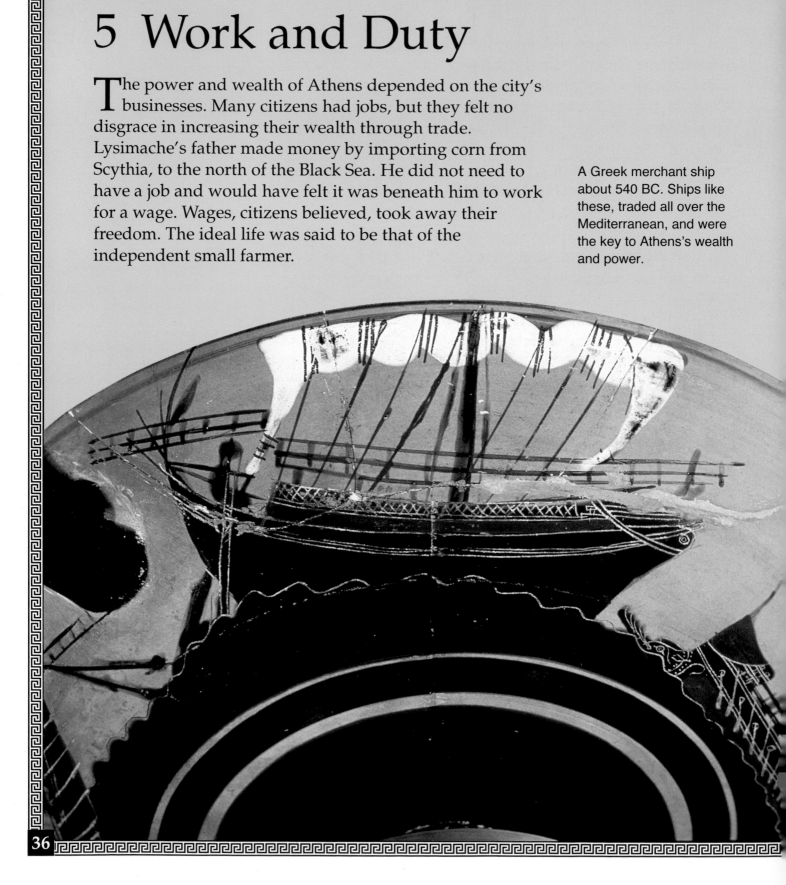

Athens's wealth owed a great deal to its *colonies*. Founded by Athenians all over the Eastern Mediterranean, the colonies provided raw materials such as timber and grain. In 483 BC the discovery of vast stocks of silver at Maronea in Thrace added greatly to Athenian prosperity.

Merchants and traders

The port of Piraeus was one of the busiest in the Mediterranean. Trading ships came laden with grain, raw materials and luxuries. They left with wine, and products from the city's many workshops.

One of the largest workshops was owned by the metic Cephalus, who employed 120 slaves in the manufacture of weapons and armour. Most other businesses were much smaller and included potteries and cloth workshops, shops, taverns and market stalls.

A silver tetradrachma (four drachma) coin from the region of Boeotia.

Money

Silver from Laurium and Maronea enabled Athens to *mint* many different coins. These included a coin with the goddess Athena's head on one side and an owl, the moon and an olive branch on the other.

The basic coin was the silver *drachma*, and there were two and ten-drachma coins too. The *mina* (100 drachma) and the *talent* (6000 drachma) were used for counting, but never made into coins.

Small amounts were paid for in *obols*. An obol was one-sixth of a drachma. The tiniest coin was worth one quarter of an obol.

'It is impossible to be a proper citizen if one does manual labour for wages.'

From Aristotle's, Politics, middle of the fourth century BC.

Φ
Χ
Ψ

ΘΙΚΛΜΝΞΟΠΡΣΤΥΦΧΨΩ

Agriculture

Hegeso's father was typical of the sturdy farmer regarded as the backbone of Attica. From his own land he produced enough for himself, his family and his slaves. He sold surplus produce in the Agora, using the money to buy goods that could not be made on the farm.

Hegeso and her family were lucky to live during prosperous times for farmers. In the previous century, most of Attica had been owned by a few wealthy landlords. Later, during the Peloponnesian Wars, some farms were ravaged by invading armies. They destroyed the vines and olive trees and ruined agriculture in the area for many years to come.

On the farm

Farmers on hilly ground kept sheep, goats and pigs. The milk from goats and ewes was made into cheese. There were not many cattle in Attica because the quality of the grass was poor.

Corn and vegetables were grown in the valleys and on the plains. Farmers tilled the soil three times a year, using a plough pulled by a mule. The corn was cut by hand and threshed by animals trampling over it. Slaves then ground the corn into flour. Some farmers also collected honey to sell in the city.

Rows of olive trees in modern Greece. In ancient times olives were associated with the goddess Athena and provided fuel and food.

'As I gaze towards the countryside, I long for peace. I'm sick of the town and miss my old village, where no one ever talked of buying and selling ...'

From the play *Archanians* by Aristophanes, about 400 BC.

ΘΙΚΛΜΝΞΟΠΡΣΤΥΦΧΨΩ

Τ
Υ
Φ
Χ
Ψ

Worshippers offer sacrifices to Demeter, the goddess of agriculture or 'mother earth'. Ancient Greeks believed that she would help their crops to grow if they pleased her with their gifts.

Vines and olives

Vines and olives were the most valuable crops. They grew best on sunny hillsides. Grapes from the vines were crushed and the juice turned into wine. Water was usually added before the wine was drunk. The ancient Greeks thought it *barbaric* not to dilute, and the mixing of wine and water at the Symposion became a symbol for balance and moderate behaviour in social life.

The oil from olives had all sorts of uses. It was used in cookery, as it is today. It was also burned as a fuel, rubbed on the body and turned into cosmetics. According to legend, Athena and Poseidon, the god of horses and the sea, once competed for Attica. Poseidon produced the horse, Athena the olive. Since the olive was thought more useful Athena won and Athens was named after her.

The duties of a citizen

Athens was run by its adult male citizens. They spent a great deal of time on their civic duties. For Lysimache's father this was hardly a problem, for he lived in Athens and needed only a few hours each week for his own business.

Hegeso's father found the duties of citizenship more difficult. He attended the Assembly whenever he could, and tried to get to meetings of his deme . Occasionally, he served on a jury service and sometimes he served as a city official.

Military service

Until the fourth century BC, Athens relied on its citizens to make up her armed forces. This meant all men had to train and keep fit. When they were 18, they began two years' military training. For the next 40 years they had to be prepared to do *military service* at any time.

Each man's service depended on how much property he owned. The wealthy joined the cavalry because maintaining a horse was a costly business. The less well-off went into either the heavy or the light *infantry*. Those with least property served in the navy.

A Greek foot soldier, or *hoplite*, ready for action. The long spear was useful against cavalry attack.

A modern reconstruction of a Greek trireme, a warship which was powered by human rowers

The navy

In the fifth century BC Athens wanted to control the whole of Greece. To do this, it needed a large army and a powerful navy. The navy was essential to protect its traders and colonies, and resist invaders. By this time Athens also used foreign mercenaries and allied troops.

The navy was first built up by Themistocles. He persuaded the citizens to use Athens' silver to construct a fleet of some 200 ships, which he led in the great victory at Salamis. As the navy grew in size, poorer citizens had the opportunity to become more important.

'*I shall bring no dishonour to the sacred arms I carry; I shall never desert my fellow soldiers; I shall fight to defend my land and its holy places ...*'

From the oath sworn by all Athenians beginning military training.

Τ
Υ
Φ
Χ
Ψ

ΘΙΚΛΜΝΞ ΟΠΡΣΤΥΦΧΨΩ

6 The Greek Legacy

An obvious *legacy* from the ancient Greek language is the many words we still use every day. These include character, music, trade, magic, star and drama. Some common prefixes (such as *uni -*) and suffixes (such as *-ology*) also come from the ancient Greek language too.

The Greek alphabet, which begins alpha (α), beta (β), gamma (γ) is the basis of our own alphabet. And where do you think we get the word alphabet from?

Literature and ideas

For centuries Greek civilization was the best in the Western World. It was spread east and west by traders, travellers and warriors, such as the mighty leader Alexander the Great (356–323 BC) of Macedonia in northern Greece. Even when Greece was swallowed up by the Roman Empire, many still regarded Greek as the language of scholarship.

'Nobody can say a word against Greek: it stamps a man at once as an educated gentleman.'

The Irish playwright George Bernard Shaw in Major Barbara 1907.

ΘΙΚΛΜΝΞΟΠΡΣΤΥΦΧΨΩ

Long after ancient Greece and Rome had fallen, knowledge of Greek was thought of as essential for a good education. Generation after generation of schoolchildren were brought up knowing almost as much of Homer, Plato and Aristotle as they did of English writers such as Chaucer and Shakespeare. This affected the way they wrote, spoke and thought.

Science and mathematics

Many of ancient Greece's finest mathematicians, philosophers and scientists flourished outside the Greek mainland.

The philosopher Pythagoras (sixth-century BC) settled in southern Italy. Hippocrates the doctor lived on the island of Cos in about 469–399 BC. Plato and Aristotle, the fourth-century BC philosophers, taught in Athens, but travelled widely around the Greek-speaking world. For a time, Aristotle taught Alexander the Great. The mathematician and scientist, Archimedes, came from Syracuse and trained in Alexandria.

The ideas and teachings of all these men, and many more like them, are still widely read and admired. They still form a part in the development of our own civilization today.

An artist's idea of what the Greek poet, Homer, may have looked like.

Architecture

The Greeks devised a distinctive style of building. It was so impressive that it has been copied and adapted by many different cultures.

After the collapse of the Roman Empire in the fifth century AD, the Classical style of architecture was not widely used for several centuries. It reappeared at the time of the *Renaissance*, which began in the fourteenth century and continued to the end of the sixteenth century. Classical architecture has since emerged in most European and American countries.

Art

The branches of Greek art that we find most remarkable are pottery and sculpture. Athenian vases, which came in five basic shapes, were the finest in the Mediterranean area. Not only were they made in graceful designs, but they were skillfully painted. In the sixth century, the pattern was black drawing on a red or orange background. In the following century this changed to red designs on a black background. Future generations of potters such as the English firm Wedgwood in the nineteenth century, have been heavily influenced by the Athenian skill.

Like Greek architecture, Greek sculpture was 'rediscovered' at the time of the Renaissance. The life-like work of Greek sculptors in stone and bronze inspired Renaissance masters like Michelangelo and Cellini.

The influence of Greek architecture can be clearly seen in the design of the Capitol Building in Washington DC, USA. It was build between 1851 and 1863.

The Birth of Venus, by the Italian Renaissance painter Sandro Botticelli (1445–1510). Venus was the Roman name for Aphrodite, the Greek goddess of love.

The Greek spirit

Perhaps the greatest gift the Greeks gave to the world was a belief in the worth of the individual human being. Although they did not extend this respect to slaves and women, they set out a framework of thinking which later cultures extended to all humankind.

Our respect for democracy, the law and human rights stems directly from the achievements of the Athenians of the fifth century BC. This perhaps helps to explain our fascination with a civilization which lived so long ago.

Items of pottery from the firm founded by the English businessman Josiah Wedgwood in the 1760s. He employed the best artists to copy classical designs from ancient Greece and Rome.

'*The mountains look on Marathon -*
And Marathon looks on the sea;
And musing there an hour alone,
I dreamed that Greece might still be free.'

From *Don Juan* by Lord Byron, the English poet who died fighting for Greek independence in 1824.

Τ Υ Φ Χ Ψ

Θ Ι Κ Λ Μ Ν Ξ Ο Π Ρ Σ Τ Υ Φ Χ Ψ Ω

Glossary

Acropolis
A fortress. The most famous is the Acropolis of Athens.

Agora
The market place in the centre of Athens.

Archaeologist
A person who studies history by discovering old building and objects found buried in the ground.

Assembly
A group of specially selected people who had the right to speak and vote on important state matters.

Aulos
A musical instrument that was a cross between a flute and an oboe, although it is usually translated as a flute.

Barbaric
Rough and sometimes cruel behaviour.

Classical Greece
500-336BC, the period after the Archaic Period and before the Hellenistic Age.

Colonies
Countries occupied and ruled by people from a different country.

Democracy
Government by the people. In Athens this meant by the male citizens.

Drachma
A silver Athenian coin weighing 4.36 grams.

Gymnasion
A room or building with equipment and space to exercise and keep fit.

Infantry
A group of soldiers who march and fight on foot.

Jury
The people who hear both sides of a case in court and decide whether the accused person is guilty or not.

Kithara
A lyre. Originally it had six strings, but this increased to seven or eight later.

Legacy
A way of thinking or a possession passed down from one generation to another.

Linen
A coarse cloth made from the flax plant.

Lot
Make a decision by drawing a name (or lot) from a selection of names put forward.

Lyre
A stringed musical instrument rather like a guitar.

Magistrate
An official responsible for upholding the law.

Metic
A foreigner resident in Athens.

Military Service
A period of time that people voluntarily or unvoluntarily spend with one of the armed forces (navy, army or air-force).

Minoan
The civilization that lived on Crete from 2000–1450 BC

Mint
A place where coins are made.

Mythology
Stories and legends.

Oracle
A place where ordinary people could consult a god or goddess through special priests or priestesses.

Papyrus
A type of paper made from reeds

Pericles
Athenian statesman and general who dominated Athens about 460-431 BC.

Philosopher
A person who uses reason and deep thought to understand and make sense of human life.

Piraeus
The port of Athens.

Pithoi
Storage jars made from clay.

Polis
A city-state and its people.

Poseidon
God of earthquakes and the sea.

Prosecute
To take legal action against somebody you believe has broken the law.

Pythagoras
Sixth-century philosopher and mathematician.

Renaissance
A revival of art and architecture from the Classical period, in the fourteenth century.

Sacrifice
To kill a beast as an offering to a god or goddess.

Styx
The boundary river of the Underworld across which the dead passed by ferry.

Swaddling clothes
Thin strips of clothe wrapped around a baby.

Trireme
An ancient Greek warship with three rows of oars on each side.

Underworld
The place where people went when they died. Sometimes known as Hades.

Time line

All dates are BC

c. 1200	The Dorian people, the last invaders from the north, come to Greece
c. 1100	First Greek colonies on the coast of Asia Minor
c. 776	First recorded Olympic Games
c. 750	Greek colonies in Italy
c. 750–700	Homer composing the Iliad and the Odyssey
c. 705	Greeks begin building in stone
c. 700	Attica formed
c. 683	Athens becomes a republic
c. 650	Classic Greek sculpture appears
c. 600	Black figure vase painting appears
c. 594	Athens' constitution reformed by Solon
c. 525	Red figure vase painting appears
c. 508	Democratic reforms in Athens
490–479	Persian Wars
490	Battle of Marathon - Greeks defeat the Persian invaders
483	New supply of silver found at Laurium
480	Battle of Salamis - Greeks defeat the Persian fleet
c. 480	Playwright Euripides born
c. 469	Hippocrates the famous doctor born
462–1 (to 431)	Democratic reforms of Pericles in Athens. The 'golden age' of Athens sees the building of the Parthenon and other fine buildings.
c. 460	Historian Thucidides born
457	Long Walls built between Athens and Piraeus
c. 454	Athens dominates most of Greece
c. 450	Playwright Aristophanes born
431–404	Peloponnesian War between Athens and Sparta
427	Philosopher Plato born
404	Athens surrenders to Sparta
384	Philosopher Aristotle born
336–323	Reign of Alexander the Great of Macedonia
c. 287	Archimedes born
147	Macedonia becomes part of Roman Empire
146	All of Greece absorbed into the Roman Empire

Further Information

Books for children:

I was there: Ancient Greece by J.D Clare (Riverswift 1994)

Eyewitness Guides: Ancient Greece by Anita Ganeri (Dorling Kindersley, 1993)

Indiana Jones Explores Ancient Greece by John Malam (Evan Brothers, 1993)

Ancient Greece at a Glance by John Malam (MacDonald Young, 1998)

The Ancient World: Greece by Robert Hull (Wayland, 1997)

Books for older readers

Greek Society by Anthony Andrewes (Penguin, 1967)

The Oxford History of the Classical World, John Boardman, Jasper Griffin and Oswyn Murray(eds.)(Oxford University Press, 1986)

Atlas of Classical History byMichael Grant, (Routledge,1994)

Places to visit

The British Museum in London has many exciting exhibits from ancient Greece. If you are ever fortunate enough to spend a holiday in Greece or go there on a school trip, do visit the museums (particularly in Athens) and sites devoted to Classical Greece. They will give you a better insight into the Greek way of life than any book!

Index

Numbers in bold indicate
an illustration.
Words in bold can be found
in the glossary on page 46.